T0381318

Top Dog

A TRUE STORY OF A LOST DOG'S
JOURNEY TO FIND A HOME

Susan Gail Davison

Illustrations by Donnie Obina

To order additional copies of this book, contact:
Xlibris Corporation
1-888-795-4274
www.Xlibris.com
Orders@Xlibris.com

ABOUT THE AUTHOR---SUSAN TRUPP DAVISON

I was born in Brooklyn NY in the mid 50's to Dorothy and Edward. I grew up on Long Island with one older brother and two younger sisters, and have wonderful childhood memories. I married my high school sweetheart four years after I graduated. I became a born again Christian and was co-founder of Christ Community Church in the beautiful Catskill Mountains for thirteen years.

I am a mother of two awesome daughters Christina Dorothy and Candelyn Barbara. I married for the second time to Anthony, a commissioned navel officer who I met in Charleston SC. I'm a very privileged Stepmom to a special Jessica Dawn and William Levi. We are a beautiful blended family, when the children were all young we adopted a puppy dog we named Sgt Major, who we all loved and bonded well with as a new family.

My hobbies are sailing, sewing, photography and gardening. Amazingly enough I won the Fem Fatale (women at the helm) race one exciting spring day with CORA, Charleston Ocean Racing Association. I currently have started "Country Glimpses" as a custom made pillow business along with photographed greeting cards of all my travels in the country.

I currently live in NY. I can be reached at CountryGlimpses@gmail.com

Top Dog

A TRUE STORY OF A LOST DOG'S
JOURNEY TO FIND A HOME

HIS NAME IS SGT MAJOR

There were beautiful puppy dogs that were born in a big old red barn in the country. One puppy was getting old enough to wonder where his family was. He said to himself, I need to find my own family. There has to be a family for me! I need to go find them. It will be a big dangerous journey to leave my brothers and sisters. I must be brave and go, or I will just be an orphan here with no family of my own.

One bright sunny morning he got up the courage to run away. It was hard to get under the wired fence. He got tangled up in the vines, and it began to get hot and he became thirsty. He took a long nap and before he knew, it was getting dark and he was getting scared. He snuggled in the woods under a tree and waited until morning to continue his long journey to find his family.

Before he was fully awake he heard someone talking, saying they see a puppy that must be lost! Oh my, said the lady with the red mud boots on. The poor puppy is all dirty and covered with ticks and fleas!

Let's take him to the animal shelter, where there could be a family for him, for he is so cute and cuddly and scared.

11

He felt happy to have so many people giving him so much attention at the animal shelter! He was settled in a cage there with food and water watching people go by as they were looking at all the dogs and cats. Most of the people that came by just didn't really notice him. because he was very quiet and all the other doggies were barking very loud.

Then, there was a very friendly lady who saw me! She noticed me because I was so quiet. Just waiting so patiently I was hoping she would pick me to go home with her. She was calm just like me! She looked at me for a very long time, but she left me there and didn't pick me. Oh I was so disappointed!

The next day the friendly lady came back! There she was again! She took me home! I was so happy. Wow! A bunch of kids lived there too. They liked me! They gave me a bubble bath and plenty of kisses too! They played with me and took me for walks in the neighborhood and I met lots of other kids too.

I was so relieved to be with my new family. My dream came true!

They named me SGT MAJOR. Wow! From an Orphan to Top Dog!

23